Francis Bede lives and writes in Tasmania

Bede, Francis
Houdini Weaned on Fear- poems
ISBN: 978-0-9806289-4-4
Copyright © 2021 Francis Bede
Cover design Francis Bede
First Published Bad Clergy Press October 2021.

All rights reserved. No part of this publication may be reproduced, stored in a retrieval system or transmitted in any form or by any means, electronic, mechanical, photocopying, recording or otherwise, without the prior written permission of the author. For information contact the Copyright Agency Limited.

Houdini Weaned on Fear - poems

Francis Bede

By the same author:

Bad Clergy – a question in five fantasies
God in the Human Machine – a theobiography

Contents

The Chance	9
The Ballad of the Melbourne Street Crier	10
Granddaddy	13
In Tongues	14
The Wilderness Photographer, Tasmania	15
Ideology	17
Sonnet	18
Fishy and Dishy	19
Suburban Pace	20
Mountains	21
Lobotomy Overdrive	23
Redemption	24
Toward Eaglehawk Neck - In three parts	25
Stammer ABBA	28
The Gag	29
The Chameleon	30
Life Architect	31
Houdini Weaned on Fear	32
Dot and Bill and Beryl	34
The Ballad of the Michael	37
Without	39

Untitled	40
When all white dots are joined to get a picture	41
Do the Shopping	42
Irrelevant Really	43
Slander Correct	44
Prunella Margarita Clitares Tonto	45
Feeding the Enemy	47
A Poem for Children	48
Human Consumption	49
Given	50
Time	51
Fic O 'Lil	52
Springtime	53
Demented	54
Broadarrow Ninety-Nine	56
The Hoon	60
Unsettled and Untitled	61
The Chomp	62
Make it Right for Me	63
Influence of Plasmatics	64
Kings Cross Whispers	65
The Promise at Twilight	66

The Turn of a Friendly Path	67
The Sculpture	68
See you around	69
Coy Glances	70
Thank you	72
Errol	74
Scratching entertainment from a pile of tinsel incendiaries	75
Her name is Alice: She is her Wonderland	77

Some of these poems have been previously published by Terror House Magazine, Leopardskin & Limes, Tinge Magazine, Oddball Magazine, StepAway Magazine, Oddville Press, Harbinger Asylum/Transcendent Zero Press, Eureka Street, Literary Heist, Mojave Heart.

The Chance

And honesty need not blush
When truth that's due, is fair.
Love may not be in a rush
When the heart emboldened,
Opens to dare.

Dare itself to take the heat
When scrutiny is around.
The pulse is a comical beat
When self-pity and insecurity,
Go to ground.

Ground away at this doubt
When rejection may be afar.
Beyond cynicism thereabout
When an open mind by trust,
Is but ajar.

The Ballad of the Melbourne Street Crier

What ho! I say to you walking passers byers, what will it be for you today?
Dips your iphones, and raise your eyses, and look see at my dispositions,
What will it be, locum lattes, curfew and piping hot, then down your pipes?
You can take it over the Flinders Street corner, and sup and sip and look,
An electric shaver you might ask, for that hairy gullet or that sad ankle.
What have I in my bag of tricks to entertain you, knob you, lest you swipe?
A screen, a screen, a parliamentary promise for a pinhead computer screen,
If that's what you want, I can get it for you, from Guatemala, it's duty free.

I'm that London Street Crier, selling all things this and that, also and besides,
You'll buy things off your shopping list, and the checkout box wouldn't know,
There'd be fine rosemary, sage and thyme, and the punchiest green mint,
I'd have a ladder up my sleeve, and if you wanted a spade, I'd have that too,
All sorts of novelties and trinkets and must 'aves and I wants it necessities.
Packets and big jars and screw-tops and containers and free-range goodies,
I'd conjure them, for a good pile of euro, or some dollars peeled off real slow,
Never takes credit, or an IOU, no need to, give me cash, hot or cold, no matter.

What's that? You want the latest, you want the prototype, you want the idea!
All right meet me on the corner at Little Bourke Street, I'll have it ready,
Interest you sir I, in a better dream than the one you have? A redundancy?
And madam what about you? Your jealousy can't really do, not in the Mall,

Hey you schoolies in uniform, can I sell you a space on the Myer's window?
Selfies are free of course. See I've got a celebrity in my second knee pocket,
An it who was an ent who was a she who was a he and ?'s name is Gender,
Had enough of confusion? They say YouTube is all the rage watching Rage.

The special's on for Dalrymple sangas and so's the flood that's gonna follow,
What's a sanga? Well might you ask, because nothin's gonna save the sauce,
Or was that Chutney? Or Tahini? Or Hummus? I'll check me multiculturally,
Something I learned about on the side streets off Tottenham Court Road,
Be prepared. Was a boy scout once. Grew up on Scouting for Boys. Grew up.
I flew here, like I was the only person who didn't need a flight attendant,
On account I had everything passengers needed in me pockets of surprises,
Customs let me through, and bought everything I had, nothing to declare.

I'll be crossing Collins and Swanston soon, and then I'll be on a paper plinth,
Bedazzling you with me finest wordies and great low sweeps of me big arms,
Fish from me pockets fish, flounder, salmon, and if I can find some, cute flake,
It's OK, I got me licence from Vic Market's fishmongers, all scrap and subtle,
Keeps it all fresh in me refrigerated pocket eskies, blue ones with white lids.
Hear ye, hear ye, all you absconders from long queues and future impatience,
I'm here to solve all your problems, every one of them, just give me a chance,
I'll cry for you and we'll cry together, and surely the whole world will too!

Once upon a time I was permanent, when I was on-call, when I was a casual,
Now you see me, now you don't. I'll pop up and stand over there, anywhere,
Me lungs are fine tuned to shout over the loudest cars and southbound trams,
When I need to, I'll inhale air from right down your town's caves and sewers,
Watch me breath though, unless you want your coffee deluxe espresso.
That's it isn't it? Something I learnt from wandering them streets of always,
None of me customers can get what they need as easy as what they want,
And I won't be hurt if you accuse me of being some covert spy from Amazon.

Granddaddy

Since the fractured dawn of yet another grandchild screaming
I've been feeling very tired,
Thick headed and wrong tongued, for my youth I am mourning
To be relevant, only to be relevant.
As limbs slacken, my bowels go on strike, preoccupying this mind,
And when is all the love I've shown to be requited?

My breath's perfumed with toxic waste; eyes crusted with sleep
And heavy is this heart of mine
Such is my loneliness, most powerful now that I am old,
Dismayed as my life is nearing its end.
And all my scratching to sooth psoriasis, not fate's happy ending,
What do I know of the genesis of pain, skilfully actuated?

Thus bowed and bent, my body spent, my semen totally dried
Gums flared, teeth rotten, my dermis long seasonally fried
Grip weak, hair thinned, veins bulging out of slack muscle
Back bent, wallet empty, face looking like a slab of gristle;
This Granddaddy was the son of the son of the son of the son
When his life had just begun.

My body of insecure balance, in a giddy sway before the edge
For this is my only complaint.
Tears of frustration flow from fissured eyes and give some relief
Though my woes insult all other woes.
My skewed thoughts articulate like arthritic mind control
Is this the reward for a saint, so cunningly predicted?

In Tongues

Speaking in tongues we confront our maker
With the conviction we must confide in him
By our rabble gabble and unintelligible hammer
Of words, mixed together in a dysfunctional mess
He sees us humbly bowed, to enthusiastically impress
We are roughage, waving "We Love God" on a banner
And then he caught me whilst miming a hymn
Suspecting I am not a giver, but a taker
I'm neither, but a constant underwriter
Of righteousness and concordances on a whim
A fortuitous leader of souls on our earthly slammer
Sexual people who live under maddening duress
And they willingly seek my loving caress
When I conduct my redemption in a holy manner
Ever sensual, these souls stranded on a limb
Who might otherwise label me as your earthly faker
We of fallen leaves who make you Lord our raker
Speak fervently in tongues and be no less dim
You would tinker with our souls, spiritual spanner
And respect us as we are, more or less.

The Wilderness Photographer, Tasmania

Ages had I left my urban concerns
in Augusta Road and I am weary;
These are hard days in the open wild,
days of solo trekking and scouting
but I am closer to my destiny:
I take my bath in Lake Salome,
guarded by the Walls of Jerusalem
carved and filled from the urges
of a timeless earth, and veins
beneath button grass which flow,
as with mountain waters, to create
no feeling more sensual.

In the disquiet of my washing I
hope the wild eyes that watch me
bear no pity, but see my life as
one scarcely fulfilled unless I am
embraced by the land's solitude:
the values of this wilderness
course in my blood, as I hope
for a sane new world, and wild
visions enter me through my
lens, and I might capture an
essence, so that each pixel might
have in it a soul.

I know I'm soon to be relieved
of my worldly weariness, for I
have tried for too long to create
a love of wilderness, and to take
thoughts away from television and
to send them straight to here;

For this is a landscape swathed
by the peripheral – the winds, the
rolling clouds and clearing skies,
to make life as vivid as the cold
I now embrace, the unsettling
beauty of it all.

Ideology

Who shall tell us what ideology is?
Not the women in their playgirl suits
Wandering the streets of whore
Waiting for a suicide refrain
To ring in their ears for eternity.
They have those sores on their arms again
The ones mined by their pubic crabs
Migrating for the summer
Escaping punishments inflicted by pimps;
The ones wearing free-range fur coats.
Nor is it in tag lines infecting buildings
The type dubbed post-modern architecture,
Nor in delinquents bashing a coke machine
Full of twisted coin, unkind legal tender.
Let them be ready for an archangel's party
The calling to home of the doubtful good
It's not abnormal for them to bleed together.
A proclaimer defiantly wears a tight wedding dress
His dried semen embroidered in the white linen
It's not abnormal ideology for him,
Someone has to wear the designer label
For zealots to find remnants of colour-blindness.
How it is that sunshine must be bottled
And bled out of pinhole punctures
For the needy desperate to watch themselves
Shake the dead hand of a drug man's mule
And expect no gift of a silver coin?
'Sunshine is for everybody' the Bible says
'For everybody living and for a price.'
It's the way the world has brought itself up:
And briefly, the best ideas are born
From breakfast cereals shaken to death
On a lonely Sunday morning before
The church bell rings in the believer's welcome,
And who shall tell us what ideology is?

Sonnet

More intense than a lie, darkened by its very nature, a swamp
This spirit's hunger stalks any positive regard for the self
Temptations easily given into, hardened into a knob of want
So down goes the addict, deeper into the bog of poor health.
Sometimes revived self-hatred, shame and anger filters it:
Yet held up scourged, inner weakness makes it transparent
The wounds are deep; what is left of self-esteem and wit?
Clearly not enough to recreate the caring parent
The promise of a habit's death is closure for the addict
Is there no greater incentive than to mount this lofty peak?
Perhaps a final opportunity to replace gaps despair hath edit
Yet don't hesitate poor soul, and leave it to next week!
  Beware, self-doubt lingers, a violent scourge of the will
  And for all this latest self-examination, success maybe nil.

Fishy and Dishy

First taken is a piece of word-fish, four syllables in size:
It will be boiled and cooled for a goodly hour
Then will its language be removed extra close
Stuffed then with cloves of mellifluent flavours
And made like a pie with salt and mint
And with chopped pauses and semi-colons
Its top pastry holed to let the hot steam out
And well cooked when conversation is served
Along with a lubricating brown ale
The chatter will be like sauce very thick
The embarrassments discarded like leftovers.

Suburban Pace

So goes an angry looking freak, walking like a murder Suspect,
Past the stroller baby's bending mum, caressing her little Need,
This sunny Thursday morning, across a city's pedestrian Mall,
Those nights of ram raiding, after kicking and a bully's Bash,
Bring in newbie days of worship, credit cards and plenty Cash,
And mobile phones go a talking, speaking ever so Spesh,
Soon glassed-up lattes are served, and moistened pastries Melt,
Near grubby pavements stood on by tribes of jean-tight Boyos,
Wary of eyes and arms of constraint; not so heaven Sent,
Their chicks mulling over sexual moments never really Meant,
Peaceful shoppers glancing, disturbed by olden Memories,
Of youthful rebellion in paisley days of sexual Revolution,
On this brittle morn, a busker sings of golden pagan Times,
When blue waters shimmered, greatly vast and mysterious Deep,
When the powers of candescent nature ruled over one and All,
Before nature's aura was scuttled, as wicked prophets Intended,
Sacred mountains shot above the scum, Yahweh's lofty Peaks,
The post-punk freak drops money into the poet's barmy Case,
Difficult times awaken while consuming masses go to Sleep,
Lunch-timers eat to the violence of the walker's angry Pace.

Mountains

When I write
I think of that
bent poet's line,
'while others are
sleeping I'm
lifting a mountain
with rivers of poems
running off'.

I'm squatting on
A black cloud
Over Melbourne,
And I only get
down
by Lightning.

I'm usually up
There because
I'm lonely,
And I often miss
The last train
out of
Spencer Street.

I like clouds,
I feel safe
In them,
and I can walk
around naked,
And no one
Can look at me.

I'm in my
Clothes now,
People can look
at me.

I've got
this sty
And I look away
when I order my
McMuffin and coffee.

And this girl I met
Said she liked me.
She bought me
A scarf,
I couldn't even
Thank her
And ran away.

If I'm destitute
I pay the rent,
If I'm insane
I converse with
them,
And all is
Not lost.

The dam is dry
down this way,
There aren't many
mountains,
But I'm trying
because it's
All I've got.

Lobotomy Overdrive

Processing data seconds in, hours out,
The mind shrinks to the size of a retarded slug,
The fight is gone…all gone.
Entering a lobotomy overdrive
Drowning in my own quicksand
Shouldn't see my bones…. Too wasted.
What's wrong with me…wrong!
I look up from my state of drudge
And see a planet eyeball gazing at me, staring at me,
Knowing on its way when it looks through me,
And sees another data worker and another and another
'Till it comes to a wall and sees
Nothing except its own dementia.
What's going on here? Eyeballs everywhere!
Red, steaming, looking for an accusation
"Look here slug you ain't nowhere"
I am catholic and yet an overstatement
There's no sense in this prosecution
No Dada…no Dada
I am a warrior. Fight on. Fight on.
Fight strong and the weak will pass
Through the eye of a needle
Quicker than a camel's fart.
No sense in waiting for a result
$2+2=5 \frac{1}{2}$. Where did the five come in?
Feel like crying a river of sand
Buck up Rogers it's nearly five midnight
Loaded and true I'm ripe for the 'morrow.

Redemption

Whilst lecturing the faithful on the evils of relationship hazards outside the bounds of god endorsed matrimony,
Who fear and dare not move beyond their directed lifestyles knowing that the genitals of the wayward reap no peace,
From herpes and syphilis and other diseases beyond god's mercy,
Be it homosexuals, adulterers or teenage romantics who defy the logic of the ecumenical commands that serve the people to perfection,
Amid the dire warning of the putrid consequences of ignoring or defying the word that both serves and commands the people,
Whether it is temporarily in purgatory or permanently in hell's fires eternally licking at the wayward anatomy and singe pubic hair,
For the infinite mercy of god has its limits and cannot be expected to tolerate the bad behaviour of the educated and blessed that should know better,
Amid the compassionate cries for the ignorant souls and the mentally afflicted who touch their private parts and know not why,
Amid the violent call for sinners to denounce all human evil and its vile manifestations,
Whilst delivering such scripted diarrhoea from the open bowels of Satan himself,
The disturbed preacher began his personal redemption.

Toward Eaglehawk Neck - In three parts

Part 1 - Caesar of the Dog Line

I am Caesar of the dog line, laid across the Neck
Hungry and raw, I await special visitors
Men they are, human wrecks seasoned with blood
No lovers of the attentions of cruel inquisitors
They come to meet me, and my fellow maulers
To cross us and seek the calms of Storm Bay yonder
Disgraceful creatures they are, mirrors to their remains
They're lives for theirs to blight and to squander.

Our fearsome gaze made enormous by great lamps
Is cast hither and thither through dark night, damp day
These men who've fled the Commandant's stone camps
Had fought through the scrub ready to pay
With their lives; for we are in no mood for bolters
Petty thieves, brigands or other foul labels
They think themselves precious, strong in life's wagers
Fools to believe life is like morals of old fables!

I sense his arrival under this salty dawn, poor blighter,
I'll get 'im Ugly Mug, I'll take this wretched eel
And toss 'im on his side; show 'im my full yawn
Tenderly first, whilst his heart spins the Wheel o' Life
Then I'll snap 'im and tear out his screams,
Word'll go back down that signal line
Another poor wretch has met 'is maker
In the jaws of zealous Caesar;
Lover of fine sinew and victim's wine
Bane of foolhardy men who break the penal law.

Part 2 - Redman the Forger

So 'ere I am a lag on the run, from O'Hara Booth
No less
Made a bolt I 'ave for freedom, sweet freedom
God bless me, I'm badly cut up by this scrub and rock
Ah, but I smell the sea, and I taste it like freedom
I'll be 'ome for Christmas and see me old mum
The Neck is close, mustn't drop down on meself
Keep it up old boy, yonder is the key to home
Think of the wind blowin' out full sails
For dear old England, for dear old Camden Town
I'll get my revenge; tog'd out to the nines
McCracken won't know me; I'll crush his skull
Poor me! What a pitiful wretch!
That slimy soup-water's given me the runs
The dogs are baying for convict blood
Never mind, I'll turn up some trump.
This is my out and out push for Xanadu
Beyond the dogs and chains in my iron black cell
What if I can't swim past these ferocious mongrels?
And what of the constables who rouse their hunger?
Prancing pretenders, flattering the young lieutenant
I cannot bear them, horrid crawlers
Here I am at a stalemate, is it freedom or death?
They be the same thing, I'm sure of it!

Part 3 - The Commandant

Rode early to the Neck with company-
the dogs are baying-
Redman must be nearby-
I cannot comprehend his need for escaping-
should these men do my bidding-
they would do well for their future-
they alone are the ones they kid-
he'll not escape into the wilderness-
everyone should know of Redman by now-
yet I would not like the dogs or sharks to get this man-
he doesn't appear to be particularly bad-
"Let us get to the Neck in haste"
no need for this man to be waste-
perhaps upon capture he will rest his ambitions-
my Nag and I ride past Stony Point-
we sense the din of Pirate's Bay-
what a gloriously pure day that has begun-
what beauty blesses this foolish act?-
wait on Nag we must attend to this deed-
the dog's welcome not only us-
what will be done for this man I wonder-
for I have other pressing needs to attend to-
Young Macgregor has given me his report-
It is time to do no more than wait-

Stammer ABBA

I nearly met my doom on Countdown Boulevard-
Four wholesome Nordics came toward me arm in arm-
Singing songs of love and sweet redemption-
Two blond boys and two handsome girls-
Their bell-bottom trousers sway in rhythmic disco-
The screams of young fans blow in from wild seas-
Even Lucifer has got that disco beat!
And songs of hope seep from beautiful lips,
The girls deliver them with swaying hips,
The boys in beards look on with total love,
Mamma Mia! The fame fits like a soylent glove!
The insane attention, the parodies are sure to come,
Their music is a disease, even for the dour,
Even for the witches who boil up trouble.
As I come closer, they spring me looking glum,
"Why pray sir do you look down on your cheer?
Our music curdles air; we make crazy cream,
Together our fans we have a whole lotta fun,
Come taste us, we fulfil your Molly's dream."
I was surely tempted but decided to move on,
For fear I'd be totally tongue-tied,
To forget I once had a vocabulary,
And forever stammer my only word – ABBA.

The Gag

Too late the comedian's gag
Has blistered in the heart
Of his victim, now bulging
With eyes deep beetroot red
And veined like an estuary
Flooding and off course,
A suited member of
An elite power group,
Whose message is
Embossed on official paper
Posted on secret doorways
Leading to corruption,
Of a kind become cliché
For none speak up
And take the long line
Like a man, not the mate
Who is weak in group-speak,
Afraid of the exposure;
The comedian tried
The victim drowned him.
Who shall step up
And take up the mantle?
Take the fight to folly
And not be put off
By sewn lips, vice scalded.

The Chameleon

Before the crowd the chameleon speaks
Of threats around and undemocratic thoughts
Of heavy jowls in the ozone hole
Of starvation, and war monger's bleats.
The crowd listens to this radical whim
Nod in agreement as his words bode grim
All shout to take up this chameleon's cause
Yet threaten no action until finding him.

Life Architect

During a three-day carnival of name tags
Aware, the delegates were not yet alarmed
The smokers' everyman cough
Relegated to gutters
After a fibrous breakfast
Scoffed.
Buckling intestines
And smelly air
Are forced by laughing.
A life architect searches delegate's eyes
To get inside the modern ape
To analyse fat and sugar content in bodies,
Cholesterol, fence feuds and climate change,
Blood pressure and other threats to longevity
Symbols of vulnerability
Written on a black board with white marker
In dot point,
Read in silence.

Houdini Weaned on Fear

Houdini weaned on fear, is sure trumpet
Grand herald, or a cyclone blow back:
Jolted flimsy windowpanes, the aftermath
Courage and mind-sap; on yer mate!

Lumps of landmass, outback camping
Obese with sandbags, the wind carnage:
There yer go mum, on board the last car
All the way down to Asbestos Town.

And tarry top green timbers do split
Flattened trees draped in mud frost:
Go home son, go home by tube-way
Hide under basement, hide the beer.

A noose around tourisms battered
After all, this landsteamer runs real wild:
The tropical victims quiver silently now
Around their crayfish, water spoiled.

The 'clone eyeball cycles in hailstones
Scrapes topsoil with its scooper teeth:
Weave the big wet, lost in road jeopardy!
Hung out wet carpets, corners in air.

Who'd ride a wild brumby like this!
Lucky the earth wheezes after desire:
From the storm floods should come
A sad dowry for the suburban dream.

Frantic mouse pointers clickety-clack
And the spines of computers curve:
Winds that blow an eclipse backwards
This is so silly, this waterfall rain.

Perpendicular objects flout thick air
Loose tarps flap like gossiping lips:
Tin house sheets swoop like plovers
This mountain adobe, a cyclone wall.

Next year in the winter solstice
Next year insurance comes knocking:
Grey suits and red ties, 46th floor shoes
The disaster drained with a signature.

Dot and Bill and Beryl

No social analysis will make much sense of Mrs Palmer's life; she who lives in a very nice clean unit in a block of ten,
She's Dot to her neighbours, quiet and respectful, no bother, helps out when she can, the neighbours are nice, they look out for each other,
Beryl across the way goes to dialysis 3 times a week, stoic she is, it's hard doing it, too old for a new set of kidneys, but she's not in a wheelchair,
Old Bill next door gets on by on a war pension and the one leg he's got left,
can't lose any more otherwise I'll be legless he laughs choking on his joke, the prosthetic hurts sometimes,
it's a good day to you squire when the power guy comes around to check the meter,
and a good day to you Bill and Dot and Beryl, the elderly are always polite,
not many strangers come here, come a few times and they're strangers no more, we've got ways of getting you to talk a little while you work, or whatever you're doing,
sometimes the community car will pick them up and take them to Friday bingo,
the first time together was when they found out about each other liking bingo,
been liking it for years they all said, one by one by one, all together now, we'll have fun get tired then we'll all go to bed, all together now, all together now,
ah you know you've got to have a vice otherwise the priest'll have nothing to pray for, no one laughs,
Dot's got two of her granddaughters staying; they don't half not clean after themselves, knickers lying around in the bathroom,
But I love 'em, their mum's not too good, and their dad hasn't been home for awhile,
One legged Bill hasn't seen his son in years, wouldn't know what he's up to, thinks he's got a family somewhere,
Beryl's lucky, her daughter takes her to dialysis, she's too tired to do much afterwards, but they have a cup of tea before her daughter has to scoot off and pick the kids up from school.

Mavis across the way died recently, such a lovely dear, had quite a doll collection, some real collectibles, the kids probably got rid of them, and the rest of her belongings she's had for years, didn't mean much to the kids I'm afraid,
It'll happen to all of us, if it doesn't fit in a mobile phone then we don't want it they'll say, the op shops can't keep up with it,
Nothing for Bill to worry about, he's donating his stuff to the Salvos when he carks it, can hear the groans, reckons he's not far off it, he's had enough of life,
What's wrong with young people today, they want something for nothing, they want it now, they want it big, they can't wait and appreciate it, and the bad manners,
Don't talk about Vietnam to anybody under 40 says Bill, they'll just say war what's it good for?
and I say for freedom and they say, what's war over there got to do with our freedom here, they just don't understand, no respect,
Beryl lost her husband in Vietnam, left with three toddlers, never married again, Bill proposed to her once, sort of serious, sort of joking,
Dot took him aside and said she'll never get over the grieving, like Queen Victoria never did over Albert,
Bill will hope 'till his last breath, don't like being alone, find it really hard to look after meself, don't want any carer coming over and snooping around,
Can still wipe between me sagging butt cheeks though, muttering to himself,
Can't do without one, says Beryl, can't expect my daughter to do everything for me, she's got too much on her plate as it is, what with one of her sons being autistic,
Dot misses her husband Joe, but she doesn't say so, childhood sweethearts they were, never left each other's side until Joe went into a nursing home,
When he started showing signs of early onset dementia she changed her life for him, did everything for him until it wore her out, broke her heart that she couldn't look after him anymore,
She's still got her car but she doesn't go far, she's eighty-two soon, on a restricted licence,
See her pulling out of the block of unit's driveway, turning left, she's going shopping like she always does on a Thursday morning,

Gets some things for Bill and Beryl, she'll ask them before she goes, not too much though, just the basics,

The rest of the week is pretty quiet for Bill, especially summer, the cricket's a bore, can't wait for the footy to start again; this'll be the year the Demons get the job done.

The Ballad of the Michael

In these modern times, the politically correct,
Meant the bad word ugly had to be replaced
By a softer phrase to ease the terrible hurt
Of the many victims who copped this barb
Between the ears, for they were challenged
So came the phrase of beauty challenged
And an odd segment in time came to rest.

There was born into this safer world a boy
The Michael, who's alarming looks resembled
The unfortunate face of the Elephant Man
Extreme surgery was out of the question
In total horror his parents felt repulsion
The boy knew he was an object of repulsion
And so began his deep need for a quest.

His lambent eyes of conviction came to shine
Like a peering sun that lights a window
And falls upon the only lovers of his presence
His parents, thus hypnotized sought his love
More than parents would of their only child
Barely three yet somehow more than a child
One who chose to be their honoured guest.

At school, and before he'd turn thirty-three
On the sporting field and at his work places
He'd suffered the asides, the taunts, the jokes
And he'd felt every knife wound aimed at him
Every bad word, and the banned word ugly
But he knew deep inside that he wasn't ugly
And all of this was part of an endurance test.

Many fell for his beautiful eyes and they loved
And spoke passionately of him in his journey
From silence to the newest saviour of the world
They rallied behind him and gave him audience
Showing admiration for his amazing courage
How he looked, said something of great courage
Which suggested he was exclusively the best.

He became world president, a sensational god
Who walked this earth and meant what he said
And fulfilled promises through his lustrous eyes
The world for a time became a happier place
He was neither sexual, nor of wanton needs
They were very simple, his earthly needs
Confirmed by gODSOn etched upon his chest.

Came a day when he walked with his disciples
Down the highest street in the highest of lands
And said a child to its mother "He's darn ugly"
Like a deep mist that had ascended a late morn
The mass of people fell out of love with this man
Could not understand why they believed the man
Attacking him as though a plague-ridden pest.

For all the great work poor Michael had done
It was for nothing, but a faithful few who recall
The times this great man had made a difference
To their humble lives and how they felt uplifted
By someone's light shining beyond his ugliness
Over peoples who behaved with gross ugliness
Who appeared devoid of belief's natural zest.

Without

I went to a movie at a cinema complex
Found myself involved in a passion play
Was I the object of the leading man's ire?
Did I arouse the lead actress's desire?
Was I the bad guy meant to behave badly?
It was a Hollywood film full of irony, sadly.
I knew I was lying on the cutting room floor
To remain a great unknown to the world.
I left the cinema feeling gutted and empty
In a car without a street,
As a scent is without its musk,
Like a sunset without the dusk,
Like an answer missing its question.
And headed for home without a house
I entered my bedroom without its bed
And lay on my pillow without my head
I awoke from a sleepless night
Moved my bowels without the meat
Had a hot shower without the heat
After eating my cereal without the milk
I stepped onto the footpath without its city
Made my way back to the cinema-less screen;
Anyway, anyhow, perhaps or but
I'll be waiting patiently for the director's cut.

Untitled

Larking pumps the heart, no sweeter breath,
Closest living, farthest passing;
Opulent joy under glandular sunshine,
Children at play, mocking death.

When all white dots are joined to get a picture

The food on the dinner table
is from the artist's palate.
And all the ochres
the reds, the blacks, the yellows
are edible for the gentleman investor
seated at a conference table, ego explicit,
His armpits perfumed with desert sweat.
The hungry galleries
have sent agents to skate red dust
to find meaning,
it shall be extracted,
and then nourishment
shall be finished off,
when the dry carpetbagger
buys the wine.
A vintage red
close to the artist's age.

Do the Shopping

Part of the trouble for everybody living is knowledge
And what openings there are for dissenting people
Why the disturbance that makes someone go wild
Why occasionally experience can be left alone;
Yet sometimes… actually it is inevitable
One must go off and do the shopping.
And to do it best is to contort backwards
Send the head through the pavement
Drag it behind, only inspecting shops
When the emergency button is hit.

Irrelevant Really

A forerunner to the hands-free mode
He's got an obvious disability
Born a thalidomide baby
Does he feel sorry for himself? Maybe;
He's often faced with the inability
To do things long armers take for granted;
The five-fingered salute is down to three.
He bends a little lower to take a pee.
And his hand-written words are a scrawl,
His driving is a high-tech brawl
Of gadgets and modified brakes,
He half stretches when he wakes,
But all this is irrelevant really.

Slander correct

Unequal in your mind's sound orb
Is the servant leaning over to say

An apology is inevitable now.
A friendly newspaper is able to print

The spelling of the victim's name
In exactly the same manner as yours.

So none may suffer out of turn
In your social media loathe to invoke

The spirit of an Oscar Wilde
Infected from lying in a filthy gutter.

Prunella Margarita Clitares Tonto

Terrible. That's what they think of my thinking.
I'm too loose. Like a kangaroo fumbling for change at a car wash.
See. They think that I'm some marsupial not fit for conservation.
I used to have a lot of friends. At school.
That was twenty years ago. When I was as popular as Carrie.
Since then, I've been a narco sissy, an amp fit for a mine. A coy cane.
And who are they I'm talking about?
They are. Burning yellow plimsolls.
That's what I call them to their backs when they walk away from me.
Unhappy.
I never made them unhappy. Never did. Never would. Just because.
I'm a simple plot. I do what's been told to me in numbers.
I'm smart. The numbers are complex algebraic symbolically.
Sometimes the craic come over to get me to muck up encryptions.
Do them in and take them to the nearest crèche.
There's one just around the corner from my digs on Beasley St.
I have to stoop to get out. My lovers crawl to get in.
That's the kind of power I have over people. I'm a blanket.
Not any old one. An Indian one with patterns.
They represent me. My totem. My myths.
They who think my thinking is terrible don't understand me.
They can't. I'm a minority without a global voice.
I tried a community centre once. I only needed once.
The bouncer took one look at me and asked me to bend over.
What for, I asked. Because I like you, he said.
And I said I didn't, and walked away.
Walked like an Australian. Beat that eh.
Walked like an Australian on the biggest street in the biggest city.
Nobody's done that. OK Tin Man did. But that was years ago.
Before internet history. Before time wandered into daylight saving.
They cut nights in half these days.
That was while I was a shifter work.
The bottom half of me was always asleep.
The manager didn't mind. Only needed my arms to stack.
I've got four. Borrowed two from a centipede squatting for a time.
Said it came up from Alabama. It was looking for a relative.
I said I didn't know any, but did it mind if I borrowed....

No problems. Truth be known it didn't need as much to get around.
Funny thing nature. It doesn't have any rules. Not really.
Sometimes when I'm bored, I give it some.
Like if it's cold outside I'll go to the supermarket in a toga.
A black one. My pocket's a shopping bag.
Just put the cereal in here love. Shopper card? Nah.
Like I said. I'm misunderstood. Should've been a chemist.
Or plant a lemon tree upside down sideways in a local park.
Hard to plant horticulturists warn. They need a lot of water.
It takes time to con cent rate the results.
And the secret is to put a sign up for dogs to piss here.
The big method. Dubbing the doggy's cocked leg.
The owners show the way.
It worked and a park ranger from Way Out West headhunted me.
Pine forests were dying on her watch. It could mean her job.
I changed from a black toga to a red cape.
Flew out pronto. Get this, her surname was Tonto.
Prunella Margarita Clitares Tonto, the 49th in line.
I liked her. Was glad to help.
She was the mother of ten children.
Sadly, I couldn't be one of them. I'd like a mother.
This could go on until I find one. This talk.
That's what they think of my thinking.
This talk that's a distraction from purpose.
That's why my centipede drop in doesn't stay out.
It has a train to catch. That was in two days.

Feeding the Enemy

I asked a member of this violent mob
Strafing the streets with firebombs,
What are her modern appetites?
And she looked at me with eyes of fire
And told me I should be proud
Of all like her, who, on their days off,
willingly step inside
their enemy's digital minds,
to twist and snipe and smack the folds
of cells manufacturing erroneous thoughts
in the accumulation of psychic data,
skewing the information that's been collected,
revealed by her in her acts of street rage.

A Poem for Children

Do you know children, you will be adults come a bright tomorrow?
And what could you be thinking of, that you should beg for or borrow?

Why, fantastic stories in books old and new, even in books electronic.
When a story captures you, your wild thoughts will be going supersonic.

Mum and dad and grandparents will ask you what you've been reading.
And you'll say it's an exciting tale, and you don't know where it's leading.

But come back later when the story's winding and wending.
You'll smile and sneak them a peek at the startling ending.

And mum and dad and your friends will be impressed by your tale.
They'll want to read all about the wild adventures of a fine blue whale.

Books are what gives you kids a healthy and strong imagination.
Fairy stories and tall tales, and myths for your keen fascination.

And you will begin to think about the world's wondersome features.
And who will ask you about them? Your parents and your teachers!

Go to bed each night, snuggle in, and cosy up to a beautiful book.
Sinbad may be there, Bunyip Bluegum or perhaps Peregrine Took.

Harry Potter or The Famous Five will never lead you astray.
So many wonderful stories you can read, early night and early day.

Human Consumption

Big fat thighs of suddenly fried
CHICKEN
Lip smackin' home-style cellulite
DRIPPING
Heart stopping clogged up arteries
CHOLESTEROL
Pre packed community life source
SLAUGHTERED
Senseless and confused in masses
NAKED
Skin seared by consumer napalm
COMPRESSED
A priori food stock
FIT FOR HUMAN CONSUMPTION.

Given

For conformity, in matters of survival
Thus I, in stereotype do please
Myself in manga speak,
Clever designs, and literal revival.
I am complex
It's time to be punished
Time to repent
Rebels are by Lucifer sent
Labelled and faction driven
Polled and market researched
By freedom, all too given
Burdened by belligerence
Nous? Dead like common sense
Life is tense.
God hangs his elbows
Over the equator's picket fence
Gossiping with mortals
Redesigning portals
For departing followers.
He's not done with
Hope and Glory
When war is ever so hoary.

Time

Our money is often wasted, so is our time
Not a crime for this is life
And my wife agrees with me
We can see in our old age
That our rage has more personal roots
Our Docmarten boots are but enough
Life is rough and our die is mysteriously cast
How we last, how we found our neighbourhood
Because we could, accorded by the rules
We aren't fools my wife and I
We will die in peace, possessed with knowing
A reasonable glowing from our heart's essence
Because our presence.

Fic O 'Lil

Fic O 'Lil, the limey shrieked,
Thy five-year-old hath truly speaked,
Och grammar! You pathetic loon,
Get thy tongue from silver spoon.

Thy cousin the Famous Sewer Rat
Hath dignity and your measure that,
You who speaketh a basic kind
In your five-year-old I hath find
Thy roots, thy ancestral glitch,
None would marry, nor would hitch
Rutted madly, spilling out babes
Left and right, Illegitimate Naves,
"Chec that spelling"; och hear it bleat
Our five-year-old hath an acid beak.

In time you might lay less with mine
Go to work and stiffen thy spine,
 Aye; and I'll be a speaker more likely,
 You're name in kind, shared politely.

Springtime

Drifts of rain drop on hunched shoulders
Of strolling eco-romanticists
Down in fogging London.
Everything is melting.
Smegma on streetwalkers
Who assault the High Street
With credit cards on galaxy limits.
It is springtime, the lord above
Smiles behind cautious sunrays
And sends sweet aromas to fumigate the bleak
In this carnal time,
When a young girl displays her breasts
Before an April flecked mirror
And behind which a young man stands.
He could touch her, but not yet
Her shyness has not fully melted.
Sun showers gliding, flighty and askance
Over soiled pavements
And traffic moves slowly enough
To leave imprints
Of tyre sweat on the overworked bitumen.
Everything is melting,
Grime of conservative buildings seep slowly
Down to the junction of wall and footpath
And lubricate revolving doors.
A bystander lingers just slowly
For his clothes to melt into spring fabrics;
Everything is melting
It is springtime and windowpanes
Distort into psychedelic faces
Pedestrians recognising themselves
Who look away.
The hours of spring lose their way
As clock faces on church steeples melt;
The minute hand shakes hands with the hour hand
An agreement to merge: Its springtime and everything is melting.

Demented

They call me demented, and they speak
Of me helpless and non-compos:
True, I am near ninety and have lived
The full cycle of life;
Their whispers of warring respect and fury
Swirl around my ears, and from whence
This reason for reproach confuses me;
I know my name, though I cannot mouth it
In the way I charged the enemy's front line
A hero in waiting, when I survived.

My deepest feelings dwell impotent
A vegetable without a mask; I sit aware
Yet unaware of life's panoramas
And sitting as I daily do, sometimes
Mouthing for a kind of relief best dealt
With by my own hand which I cannot raise;
Damn this incapacity to control destiny
For I'm a plunger toward an eternity
A peace sought after by all who believe
In the ultimate and the terminal.

How strange I'm in a bib worn when
I was a babe fed stewed apple on
A spoon guided by a sure hand to a
Mouth open for this sweet nutrition
To kick-start a life of total fulfilment
Swelled with hope and expectations;
Babe I was who subconsciously knew
Joy when grasped but ebbs away
Like dribbling and porridge from my
Gummy gawp, the blank expression.

Today I was bathed, toileted and
Clothed to be ready for a beautiful
Day of sunshine, songbirds and
Relatives in a mode of intense attention
Over this truly helpless man-babe
What a life to be. Wait! A life that was,
A life ebbing away with no reason
For this living decay, my mind snap
Frozen then thawed; a quantum
Step into a wooden box for burning.

I am demented and feebler than when
I first emerged into the world of ninety
Years or so; and mother, who she was,
Was there! I'm sure someone was there
A body like here; but no, I hear voices
Cutting my thoughts like a surgeon's knife
Into membrane, and I'm drifting under
An anaesthetic and sorrow flitters, the
Sorrow of all that is past and swoops
Like the hungry eagles on Prometheus.

Broadarrow Ninety-Nine

We the incorrigibles are on our way to be cured
Ah, but I'll tell of our crimes passionate and lurid
Rebellion is in our hearts, against a system so cruel

Sorell, your injustices has set you up for being a fool
These crimes I am accused of in Van Diemen's Land
The fight against injustice dealt me by a vicious hand

Hot lashes and dark cells shan't break my iron will
Fight I this war, fight and fight until the enemy is nil
This pathetic convict transported for seven long years

I got caught stealing a watch whilst starving to tears
Sent to Van Diemen's Land in cold shackle and chain
And arrived sober, not dead drunk or much insane

C'mon Macquarie Harbor, deal with me your worst
I'm sent to you now, vile bastard who is cursed
C'mon Hell's Gates welcome me as your own

My simmering hatred is to the marrow of my bone
Solitude and I marry into this god-forsaken isolation
My hardened heart dwells most in cold desolation

Although I'm to be contested by the Roaring Forties
I'll feel triumphant whilst planning wicked sorties
The kind to allow me sensual freedom in a moment

Subtle patience my reasoning for plans consistent
By working in this settlement and roll the Huon Pine
And test my bastard corporal be letting out a whine

These great logs appear to me to have a subtle grain
'Though not so subtle as to cause me grief and pain
But our ships should have little cause to be sunk

My weariness turns my mind into a strangest funk
A kind of dreamscape is this prison without walls
Unbreakable scrubs tease with raucous waterfalls

The waters around us flow a thickly coffee brown
Should I choose to die this way, I doubt if I'd drown
Tempted as I am, ferried from Sarah Island to work

Though the beauty of a calm day may seem a perk
I must remind myself of the colonial evil at hand
And be ready to escape and forever be damned

Time is of no consequence for it passes me by
Occasionally I pause and glance to god up on high
And pray for the day I'm to get permanent release

My head is bowed low to manage my inner peace
But unlucky others have bitten the beastly hand
And felt the cruel floggings and the grist of the land

My inner strength comes not from pastoral homily
Nor from dried pork, brittle bread or meagre hominy
But from a fierce desire to right in me these wrongs

I hope to be famous; my deeds sung as great songs
Yet this rank dreariness has deeply entered me
Here in labouring, there when I can't let things be

And it is by years, months, and days this sort of life
A cycle of desperation and hope, my heartland's fife
It is no longer this hated system but myself I fight

Not that I'm fearless just wingless to my flight
It is a tough mental attitude I am trying to maintain
Beware my godless spirit from which I must refrain

Chances pass, the time's pain and hope had wed
I'm to exert myself from spinal cord to a clear head
A rebellion in the face of authority, the squires of fear

Even as I stride half-starved, I'm stepping up a gear
Whilst working with the logs and in the saw pits
Double or nothing cowards, I'll not call it quits

Alas dysentery and rheumatism has taken hold
I look yonder and search for Frenchman's Gold
And deny that I am victim to a tyrant of distance

Although by nature I'm built for calm resistance
The lash finds my scarred back ever more regular
These cruelties have forced doubt, and I'm secular

Too many cat cuts and months of putting in spades
Too heavy the hand of my betraying comrades
I'm counting the lashings at a hundred yards apiece

My essence flows, aye, but it's not going to cease
The punishments defy reason and are out of control
And the hog's lard can't ease what pain can extol

My blood's coming to the boil in all of Hell's fury
I have secretly decided to be my judge and jury
And move away from a life of desperate low worth

Be the kind of person blessed at the time of birth
And try to exterminate the many sources of my rage
By reckoning for a new dawn, a kind of new age

Before winter's cold I'll have my children in gowns
After a working day and collected my hard crowns
Then to bed with my wife and to lay gently with her

By the warmth of memory of hard times that may stir
As my love is spent, my tears now flowing forth
In the comfort of my loving dear for all it's worth

I'd be aged thirty-two on the cusp of modern times
I shan't believe I am capable of committing crimes
Having lived in Hampstead Heath for two warm years

I'm at the Foxes Inn with mates and good cheers
Sensing friendship with bold men who aren't a threat
We'll go down to Ascot to find frisky nags to bet

My brothers and I who return from a colonial war
Have done great deeds to be written into folklore
And snap goes my foggy mind and I have to degrade

Cuthbertson's head's split by my sharpest sling blade
He's the bitterest enemy I'm borne to defeat
His bad brains squashed 'neath my bare bloody feet

So there is my swift rebellion, my impatient fellows
I'm about to hang slowly from a crude set of gallows
Injustice has fallen and I'm grateful for the triumph.

The Hoon

Cruising driverless, down a nameless corridor of quiet
The car with the heartbeat throbbing through glass
Loud…louder…loudest
The young like the style; the elders are revolted
Damn hoons flooding our footpaths with noise
These boys haven't the poise
The morals, the grace to be citizens of repute
They puke
And like all monsters who bear no remorse
They laugh
In the pleasure of knowing, quite knowing
How much of a nuisance they can be
In the car with the thumping heartbeat
Cruising driverless down the High Street after dark.

Unsettled and Untitled

Umbelliferous, pentarchy and foie
The type of words, which elevate
Obscurity into stardom;
For I, whose sculpture is chipped
By the years of frustration
Its toll by ego overdone.
The world is simple, profound
In all the tableaux of wisdom and
This revelation has none greater;
Otherwise, I have an alternative.
Pretend to be counter insurgent
And win the war of self-aggrandisement;
Glory to be, an introverted experience
In the midst of my heart, the wanting to be,
Who writes lonely beside a dripping tap,
For the rhythm
If nothing else.

The Chomp

And it was felt by a nation, a shark's chomp on a swimmer's leg.
And as he bleeds, the nation slowly withers,
For fear lives best in damaged bodies:
And as leisured minds struggle with the horror
The call went out for the shark's demise.
And the search for the criminal predator is on for days,
No sandbar was left unturned; no wave was left unspeared;
No coral reef was left unscoured;
And the sharks swam in packs, curious but wary.
The media remained on red alert,
But the one, a great white, was not to be found
And the search came to its disappointing end.

The swimmer recovered from the bite to his thigh
And the nation was relieved, and got on with life.
It is more probable to be bus whacked than be eaten by a shark
Some said;
And if one wades into murky waters at dawn, trouble is aroused
Experts said;
Shark nets are the beach citizen's best protection others said.
Those who play, people say, must respect the way
Sharks rule from the depths to a sea shore's shallows
And know the risks playing in the shark's marine grotto:
And fear lives happiest in vulnerable bodies
Its secret place behind the heart.

Make it Right for Me

When good Jesus wasn't makin' it right for me
I made a miscalculated detour unfortunately
Onto a one-way freeway of perpetual misery
And I'm drivin' my redemption horned Cadillac
Listening to Elvis and Carl Perkins on the radio
Got red-eye sunglasses to cut short the tears
Drivin' and bemoanin' my worldly troubles.
It's fortunate I have a billion barrels to burn
My Caddy's new engine hasn't missed a beat
I hope the transmission fluid stays real moist
And I curse my ex-wife for crookin' me
And my da for cold waterin' my good ideas
I feel Mr Authority workin' the insides of me
Can't find the bible verse sayin' no means no
C'mon Jesus won't you make it right for me.

Empty fried chicken cartons fill the back seat
Crushed lemonade cans line-dance the leather
No need to answer the two calls of nature
But it's flirty work hind-sightly drivin' blind
Tryin' to manoeuvre this highway of old regret
No CHIPS speedin' on bikes 'll flag me down
There's no one here to care for my troubles.
I've left my baby back in Redemption Town
And my old ma don't know I'm flyin' ragged
This god-fearin' road's makin' me feel stewed
If I'm gonna go down I'll go down disgracefully
This here cowboy's runnin' on a blade's edge
His hat's a wonky tilt sittin' on follicles all bent
Can't even pull over and say a bunch of prayers
C'mon Jesus won't you make it right for me.

Influence of Plasmatics

If, plasmatic screens arouse, if
When, controlling aside, when
How, noise turned bliss, why
When, thinking is numb, how
If, the sight disappears, when
Why, what follows light, when
Who, gnome viewers, who
How, light fades minds, how
When, sight cleared for entry, if
Why, the mind reincarnates, when
How, the air reignites, how
When, electrified moods, if:

Kings Cross Whispers

Dark sounds evoked by traffic incubi
Announce this saunterer who walks on by.
And the breath of his city will soothe him,
When he finds for himself a public space,
Or a familiar entrance; seeking companionship
In Kings Cross shops and in arcades.
He walks, forestalling double loneliness.
For he is lonely in the city world
when he walks through it.
And he is lonely when he measures himself against it.
There are no family or friends to claim him.
And there is no expectant God awaiting him.
When he saunters, his time is spared
of natural business,
of an ever-growing pulsating urban flesh,
When thousands of its wasted seconds
Scream for some syncopated air:
The breath of earth,
Infiltrates his labouring thoughts,
Of his need to belong,
Of his fighting legacy,
For he was once a soldier, then a truant.
The street's participants
Whisper at his passing.
There is too much competition on the ground,
That's what his voices say,
His companions in elocution.
When they speak, this is when he is least alone.
Whom does he love? Ian Hunter wants to know.
Voices which describe the same haggling dream
When he's scrambling over battlements
Spread along tops of streetscape walls
With Buddha faces jutting from them,
Their tongues poking out just far enough,
ready to catch him,
when he jumps,
his substance having given up its spirit.

The Promise at Twilight

As the concierge of a darkening sky brings
The stars from sister atmosphere to her brother dusk,
The colours of the evening fade and sleep.
And the black beds itself around the luminous light
Of a full moon bonded to star bright
For the creatures of the night
To lively up the still
For the dead to begin release
Their agonized bodies contorted not;
Something magical after rot
And finding a spot, where the sun
Arises with their spirits as another.

The Turn of a Friendly Path

There are semblances of him scattered
Around in old photos, postcards
Half-finished love letters;
His last excursion was on a lonely path
That of a dirt road, way out-back,
Which ends on the edge of a dried lake;
His family hopes that
He might return as though
Heavy rains in storms,
And fill the lives of those
To whom he matters most,
With his love,
His kinship,
Free from the drugs
The alcohol,
Free to yawn at their caring,
And caress the damage as though the Christ,
And bind his troubled soul
To Fortitude, to begin again.

The Sculpture

Like a naturalist I made close and detailed observations
Of a roadkill, a potoroo, fresh dead in grass,
How its death would lead to decay.
Its blood was a paint stroke on the roadway
soon to be washed away by rain.
The dragged body lay stiff in grass.
The smell of death wafted from its body.
And each day as I passed, the body swelled some more.
And it was like this for a few days.
And then the gasses burst free.
I missed seeing it happen.
And when the body sunk into itself
the decay really began
and the earth took what it needed
and the fur and the skin decomposed.
The organs decomposed.
The days of decomposing work went on.
On into weeks until there were the bones.
And like an archaeologist I took the bones,
and careful not to break anything of its structure
I took the bones home.
And like a mechanical engineer I observed the skeleton,
Observed its mechanics, observed its construction.
And like a palaeontologist I took it apart
and studied each individual bone,
how each interconnected with the other.
I studied the skull, the paws, the backbone.
I spent weeks studying
before I recreated the found bones,
Making a sculpture like an artist.

See you around

I don't need a mobile phone
I don't want one
I like my push buttons to be voluptuous
They fill my fingertips
I like the sound of the telephone ring
The way it grounds me
I don't need to see who I'm talking to
I can imagine them
Like in the fairy tales of my childhood
I don't need a call
When I'm constipated at the stock exchange
Or when I'm snogging in the cinema
I like my space
And I like the silence
The gaps in between spoken words
I'll keep my eyes open
And see what's around.

Coy Glances

In the Garden of Eden, a scene is set for two lovers, whose eyes circle then meet;
Alone and abandoned by the One and fashioned for a tumultuous future,
The One wouldn't dare guess their infinite fate, nor intrude in areas naturally intimate;
Their fumbled utterings and coy glances, bold nakedness and latent differences
Suggest the beginnings of seminal romance:

The Fella: You show discomfort yes, at my unashamed sly grin?
The Girl: Not so much as you may insist, my subtle lover to be
F: You're a smart one; you take me for a heavy fool
G: Let me guess; you my pet have little time for inner knowledge
F: In strange moments like this I have no heart to question
G: Then patience sir, is the crown of one's insistent ardour
F: I'm no SIR, I am the primal ready to take you there
G: Oh, but where my nightstick, where am I to go?
F: I'll look elsewhere if you give up on my charms
G: Meditate less on your loins; or your arse will consume you
F: I agree, there is no one else for now, perhaps not tomorrow
G: I should be happy if you are the eternal light of my life
F: For my part darkness may invoke violent discomfort
G: What with me? My heart is no place for bald inquisition
F: I have not yet asked the first question that I may ask
G: Then come to me my lover and I'll give you an answer
   Come closer, closer, and sense the fragrance of my naked skin
   Fail not your bravery and whisper only words I need hear
   My humour and sensibilities are no longer arbitrarily thin
   I hunger and yearn for you; I am nothing to fear
F: Now wait on dear; I need to make time for consultation
    And 'tis not procrastination I reckon, look at this state I'm in
    Naked and embarrassingly sexual, with not a penny for security
    No, I fear something I can't understand, I may unravel
    Turn away from this idea of myself and be lost
G: Poor boy! You have to prove it to yourself and maybe the One
   That upstate ego of yours will have you awash with sweat
   And the One knows what else!

Your loss of yourself is your gain of me
Come, consult me and possess me until we are spent!
So that we may beget our children's children
And be founders of a species, and unleash the unknown
Take me! Fear not our foul breaths as our quivering lips meet
Here, take a bite from this apple some old serpent gave me
Here, refresh yourself with me, as a play for our consummation
Of love and physique, and these first words we have forsworn.

Thank You

Thank you
For Memories lost
My minds aberrations
Have all been tossed

Thank you
For Hidden vowels
My blank verse
Has moved my bowels

Thank you
For Puppy fat
It's taken me years
To get rid of all that

Thank you
For the Desperately famed
My random spleen
Can be correctly aimed

Thank you
For Dad and Mum
If they hadn't made me
I'd be dreaming dumb

Thank you
For a Mysterious universe
Granting me the favour
Of judging with a curse

Thank you
For the Upper class
There's still a chance
They may kiss my arse

Thank you
For Anger repressed
I've strength to leave
And be not depressed

Errol

Errol had one wish to live and two to die
depending upon the interval he was at,
It's beginning, or at its end.
Then at fifty he met his end.
And in a statement read by a school of fish
They wish to express their deepest sadness
For he was a fine one on the screen.
For no man has left this earth
with an impression so well metabolised as his.
Excuse this dictionary word, the fish cannot
fully understand
Their great loss of his attention,
When he looked down at them and stared,
His moments of inner peace being rare.
The ladies, smitten by his charm,
are smitten no more, and so are the fish,
around Sirocco, rotting at its moor.

Scratching entertainment from a pile of tinsel incendiaries

Off he goes shovelling funster food into his dumpster gob
For the tenth time today
And he ain't even fat
How 'bout that!
And his praying with the drink on a humid Friday afternoon
Glass in every position
Congratulate him people
He's a wanted man!
We're looking about for an extension to his nervous tension
His feet tapping left to right
When he's standing
Simultaneously!
Thinking of turning himself inside out for our canny audience
Seated backwards
Heads bowed slowly
Patience for the bile!
When all else fails try trading in his skin for a different colour
Out there, dad is disapproving
The church; ah the church
Easy what, to show it up!
C'mon freak, unzip the swimming stuff from your scrotum
There ain't no women here
No babies to get scared of
Be damned your inhibitions!
Now he's sitting with a ukulele playing his psychedelic teeth
No notes harmonising
Like the blues going straight
What for? May you ask!
And another thing he can almost quietly and very eerily do
Don't be shocked
The type of guy he is
How he seeks approval!
Here's his ego dancing like a leper ballerina lurking speed
They're a double act
The pay gets bigger
And the manager says so!
The tensions been thrown into the playground with his skin

Nothing left but self-esteem
A sane sense of being
Some kind of purpose or what!
He's thoughtful of the audience; for they have been truly truly
Very nubile to his act
Willing to digest the news
Hey this glum guy is hot!

Her name is Alice: She is her Wonderland

A poverty of toys enriches the imagination
Of a growing child on Camden Street
Her Hephaestus eye that grows
Into stories, into character's heartbeats;
She's seen the realms of angelic demons
She's seen the clans of the Seraphim
She acts out ancient Peloponnese wars;
In chalk upon her door, she bonds epistles
She writes of Cleopatra's love for herself
She draws the patterns of wind fled sands
And sees cool light in the Hazards of Hell
And seeing too, her absent father walking
Carrying a featureless toy from a $2 shop.

www.ingramcontent.com/pod-product-compliance
Lightning Source LLC
Chambersburg PA
CBHW031428290426
44110CB00011B/568